ROOTS, REALITY & RHYME

Turiya Autry

Good Sista Ink
Portland, OR

Published by Turiya Autry & Good Sista Ink
Portland, OR

www.TuriyaAutry.com
facebook.com/turiya
facebook.com/RootsRealityandRhyme
twitter: @TuriyaAutry

ISBN-13: 978-0991327843
ISBN-10: 0991327845

Portions of this book have appeared in other collections,
periodicals & websites.

Cover design by Vagabond

Praise for Roots, Reality & Rhyme

"This warrior of light fearlessly uses words to resurrect love, hope, truth & beauty all in celebration of life."
~**Avel Louise Gordly**- activist, educator, Oregon legislator

"In this book, Turiya Autry parades through your imagination-singing, stomping & dancing with memories from the four corners of your brain."
~**Boots Riley** of *THE COUP*- artistic agitator

"At the end of the day, love will save us, but first we must confront our voyeuristic & disconnected relationship to the violence that composes our world. Turiya's poems are a meditation on the 'maimed & misplaced' dance steps that waltz us through this journey. With a woman's sensuality, a mother's care & an activists' heart, *Roots Reality & Rhyme* provides an emotional blueprint for imagining ourselves back into a gorgeously mended & full humanity."
~**Christa Bell**- artist, writer, cultural healer

"In this book there is beauty & power. Turiya's poems are like gifts that give fully every drop of their essence from the page into your mind. I imagine them as stones willing themselves into flight, from terrestrial gravity into stellar weightlessness. They fall back to the page musically only to give again with each reading."
~**Mic Crenshaw**- cultural activist, poet, educator

"Here is a poet who listened to the details of the world so much that the smallest chirps, the footsteps of ants & saints on street corners, all infuse her being. But here, too, is a witness to tears shaped like barbed wire, the shadows of a mob, plagues labeled black. Here are poems that don't flinch. Bravo, Turiya Autry."
~**Bao Phi**- author of Sông I Sing, Loft Literary Center program director

Dedications

To my beloved mother, Emma Kathleen "Kathi" Smith
(December 10, 1948- January 7, 2007)

Throughout our time together, she was my best friend, my number one supporter & fan, as well as my inspiration & confidant. I give thanks for everything she taught me & all of our memories, knowing that I would not be the person & artist I am today without her influence & guidance. She was a living example of being resilient in the face of hardship & being understanding, open-minded & loving beyond description. This release marks the 7th year of her passing. I miss her tremendously.

To Elijah & EKela

Every day I am grateful for the learning, joy, direction, laughter & immeasurable love that flourishes in my life because of their presence. I am so proud of the two of them & look forward to all that they will become. By pursuing my creative ambitions, throughout their upbringing, I hoped to model the expectation that they find & follow their dreams. I thank them for sharing me with the world & for being my worlds. They are the greatest gifts in my life.

hagar's tears & winged-horse footsteps
draw fountains forth from outcast histories
buried in battles & bodies
born of mothers' spilled blood
inspiration resurrects herself fierce
in lightning & thunder
... some learn to fly

Table of Contents

Roots

thirteen

thirty-three & a third

reality

Growing Galaxies

i awoke in breaths
tripped upon a thought
& brought myself into existence
on a warm wet night
meditated each idea into a star
then stretched one open
freeing daylight

tugging blankets of oceans
over my shoulder
i collided on land
threw sand to the seas
painted grass meadows
until i grew impatient
with the magnitude of such art
tucked myself back in the womb
to dream again

returning to starlight
i found too much white space
splashed it with rainbows
daffodils & sunsets
carved clay animals
kissed them conscious
let their running footsteps
sprout habitats
for each inclination

catching the basics of creation
life spread contagiously
carpeting day & night
with intention

meanwhile...

i explored infinity
planting planets & black holes
to grow galaxies
twisting time into spiral ropes
i skipped dimensions

then,
sketching stories & equations with constellations
across the canvas of my imagination
i decided to pull space wider, until every edge
d i s a p p e a r e d . . .

Littleton

what lurks beneath the surface
in these small towns
specks on the map
that gain notoriety
through bloodshed?

who are these children
that hide behind arsenals
build pipe bombs for recreation
externalizing the emotions
festering below the surface
of their unpopular exteriors
unwanted bodies?
silent screams of rage lying in wait
for the moment of climactic release

why are children waging war
in the streets, the schoolyard
destroying flesh without respect for the soul
stealing life like 10 cent candies at the corner store
& why are things that happen in cities
noticed more when they happen in the country?

what do we do with adolescent soldiers
killing youth for no gain
with governments at war
slaying the innocent
for borders carved in boardrooms
by the chosen few who choose not to share the wealth

does either battle have just cause
can either preach right & wrong
do they understand the difference?

what will we teach our boys
that thrive for power
but know not where it resides

searching for answers in places filled
with questions & paradox
fiction & lies
finding false manhood in destruction
fearing nothing
- but love

& the president says
we must teach our children
to resolve conflicts with words not weapons
while stealth fighters fly & schools go under funded
yet we wonder why the children resort to violence
instead of understanding

Chaos

because sometimes parents
are detained & otherwise absent
& the overworked & underpaid rarely rest
we are unable to rectify acts unjustified
& materialized in the form of our present lives

meanwhile, our children attempt to grow free
& we have no garden of eden to offer them
our backgrounds stunted by pesticides
manufactured lies & homicide
city streets causing us to travel
twice as far, twice as fast
we live at odds with the atmospheric pressures
begging folks to just "slow down!"
we cast seeds on the run
hoping something nourishing will come

chaos races unaligned
his energy gains momentum
yet seems to never topple
with the weight of itself
unobstructed
he gathers us all
into his arms
& welcomes us

Backyard Daydreams

i remember as a child imagining
if i could sing a beautiful enough song
birds enchanted would gather
whistling on my outstretched arms
squirrel sopranos singing chorus
drumming acorns on trees

unfortunately, as a mediocre singer
my attempts lacked whatever magic
such spells require

maybe the jays, robins & chickadees
looking for someone to listen
decided i didn't appear up to the task

even the trees didn't realize
they could trust me
feared i might sabotage their plans
to reclaim the landscape

i listened to them whispering
wind camouflaging their conversations
wise elders with hidden roots
mysterious beings guarding neighborhoods
playgrounds & wilderness
who witness too much
to remain silent

i assured them, "i am on your side"

i asked other children not to step on ants & spiders
bugs they didn't see reason for or feared
ants would speak for themselves
but too busy to slow for socializing
dedicated creatures move with purpose
rarely resting, unapproachable
heads down, hurried footsteps

failing to stick around
unless i dropped morsels for them

without saying thank yous or farewells
they moved on quickly as possible
in search of the lost trail home
over sidewalks, through fields of weeds

i wished them safe travels along their path

when the sun managed to find
its way back from vacation
spring celebrated the return
scattering pink & white confetti carpets
blossoms sacrificing fragile bodies
to give thanks for the change in seasons
& prayers for abundance
bright splashes of hope
amidst gray skies

i thanked the trees

providing perch & seed
to climbers & fliers
spinning room for spiders
sharing fallen sweets
branches & shade
maintaining balance
& teaching harmony
to those who listen

Rwanda I: Kibuye

when abel fell at the hands of cain
& spilled blood stained the ground
did they know they were in paradise?

when the birds share songs
lending melody to their surroundings
is their sound the telling of the way
the world went mad
or perhaps the release of joy
that those times are over?

do the buried find peace
with skeletons dismembered
lives disrupted with strokes of a blade
since bullets were considered too expensive?

when those in need who sought salvation at a church
found the house of god had become their tomb
was there redemption for those
who wielded the machete?

do adam & eve weep again
as history repeats itself?

how do we reconcile that eden & hell are neighbors
separated by a chain link fence & barbed wire
unmarked mass graves in a courtyard
sharing both sides in indecision?

is evil also a fallen seed
that takes root with barbed spikes
laying claim on man & earth
to harvest discontent?

we haphazard gardeners
consume hull & husk
choke on the yield

emaciated & forever hungry
despair masks itself as sustenance
hope lies in the hands of children
asking me for rwandan francs

but my meager offerings
cannot return their families

Playground

fearless of falling
teetering on the silver rung
she reaches for the bar
grasps cool steel between blistered palms

unaccounted for scratches & bumps
mark kindergarten length legs
which require another year to grow the distance
that now separates her from the metal cylinders

she grins
& with a quick leap
floats high above her vast domain
called **playground**

seventy-five times she travels back & forth
from one side of the bars to the other
(minus the three skipped while counting)
each pass completed with greater conviction
now that the physics of sway & release
are inherent reactions
progress self initiated

arms stretched wide as wing spans
she rests in the middle
catches her breath
legs swinging to the rhythm of her thoughts
while she surveys
the span of grassy field between fences
the twisted slide in the distance
faded red plastic glory
jutting from the pavement

scattered children chasing
throwing, bouncing balls
screaming, laughing
at play

when it happens

an object in motion will stay in motion until

boys gather needing something
to occupy/take over
controlling essentials
of youthful existence
… space

"it's my turn!"
one declares while mounting the ladder

not ready to abandon her perch she dismisses
the commands of the golden-haired boy
with fierce eyes & attitude
whose name she will not recall later

offended, he flings himself
towards the center
deciding his turn is **now!**
suspended somewhere in the middle
strong wills collide
flinch frantic mid-air syncopations

she clings tight
arms trembling from the burden of strain
holds fast as his legs force their way
around her waist & tug

baggy pants bought large
to last several seasons
slide towards her ankles
the message revealed on white panties
speaks volumes for her future
"i love you! i love you! i love you!"
in bright repetitions of red text
curving around her narrow hips

surrendering to gravity
& embarrassment
sneakers hit pavement

she flees

Now They Want to Walk in Your Shoes

we share no blood
no need to consider you sister
merely a relationship of unfortunate circumstance

we steal memories of happiness
with each insult & order
until you can't remember ever being loved

we wake to splendor & finery
while you own nothing
but the streaks of ash across your face
& dingy rags not fit for wear

      your failure defines our success
      your plainness points to our beauty

no time for daydreams
your ambitions rubbed raw
like fingers scraping washboards
with linens & laundry

we are the ones
whose dreams are destined
to be more than mere fancies

      do not be idle sister
      we are watching

how dare you find time to sing
when there is drudgery to be done
supper time is near, pleats need ironed
gowns fastened, shoes & silver polished
dishes need washed, floors mopped
socks mended...
its endless

so there will be no ball for you

no midnight dances with princes
one of us will be the chosen prize
our hands soft with pampering
dresses specially made
hair in silken ribbons
shining like spun gold

     don't wait up for us cinderella

unless your list of chores
proves long enough
to keep you working past midnight

Self-Centered

silence is not quiet
it speaks to me
welcomes a host of thoughts
loud & disturbing
harsh & sincere

silence is not quiet
it answers my questions
with spitefulness
tells me i am no more
than a days passing

but i burst at the seams
want to be the sun
& fire in the center
causing gravitational orbits
to circle my light

like moths near flame

Rwanda II: Kigali

we dig through graves
looking for answers in skeletons
femurs cannot explain the actions of a mob
skulls bring no clarity to what cannot make sense

we, voyeurs, glance at displays encased in glass
tread on well laid tiles & gray carpet
gaze at photos & videos
knowing we would never wish to be here in '94
but events are safe for us to witness as history
our interest too late to stop what's happened

we scavenge through the past wearing gloves
so we aren't infected with its rawness
sterility is a great distancer of heart & hand

i cannot look away from the pictures
those who miraculously survived
with machete wounds, missing limbs
piles of bodies, rivers of blood
mangled manifestations of division
lying haphazardly in a churchyard

i buy no souvenirs to take home
i am afraid to remember
even though I have no choice

the 250,000 buried here
demand we never forget

Fear of Forest Fires

i've loved softly
tip toes padding gently
over smoldering coals
scared to ignite
scarred from previous wildfires
charred forests undone
survivors stand as reminders
to be careful

so i love soft
stick to contained candle light
afraid to scare quiet with thunder
whispers choking deafening roars
swallowing silence, becoming thirsty
fear surfacing as doubt
in my own voice

i choose to love soft
without worry & risk
on familiar streets
away from the world
so i am not tempted
by sharp edges
& desires to run with scissors

like absent kisses
forgotten memories
& truant conversations
diluted by indifference
pretending less investment
promises less loss
i've loved soft

Black By Definition

the mirror held her captive

she searched from the deep dark coils that framed her face
to the blemish that was making its way to the surface of her chin
left profile- right profile, she shook her head in disbelief

could it be true?

delicate fingers forced the medicine cabinet
open for umber eyes to inspect
there was no trick or perverse optical illusion
distorting her reflection
the mirror was genuine

this realization brought her crashing
at the doorstep of a major dilemma:
if she was black, as her reflection bore witness to
what did that mean?

she didn't need a dictionary to define black
her world screamed out in immeasurable decibels
the negativity of such a color
black: the color of death & destruction
plagues labeled black, evil-doers wore black

black: the imminent force
making people afraid of closets & spaces under beds
hostile, cruel, the impending doom before an explosion
a menace corrupting the country
the color of curses & the damned

no amount of ivory soap & elbow grease
could remove the stain covering her body
she descended into a dark depression
overcast emotions found her lost
in a night without moon or stars
treading on soot amidst an ominous backdrop of despair

19

a land of evil intentions surrounded her
there was no hope here, only darkness
but somewhere in the distance
she saw a light & moved towards it

blinding white enveloped her
glistening snow danced in the air around her
ice castles reached towards marshmallow clouds
sweet tastes of sugar crystals filled her mouth
doves alighted upon her shoulders cooing
the perfection of such a peaceful place
rosy-cheeked, blue-eyed angels radiated purity & love
sang of innocence & goodwill

could this be heaven? could this last?

the gleam of whiteness faltered
transforming as lightening flashes split open the sky
white sails blowing in the winds of colonialism
came rushing towards her

she saw the white of shark's teeth
following behind to devour the countless bodies
thrown overboard in atlantic crossings
long white rows of nameless tombstones
marking the graves of the conquered
fields of white cotton tinged with the blood of weary hands
men hiding behind white hoods
terrorizing during knight rides

white: the color of a burning cross & a false god
white: the lies told by politicians before elections
white: the color of surrender

then came another set of images, a myriad of color
gold pyramids rose to meet the sun
peacock blues & cadmium reds adorned great pillars
covered in picturesque writings
brilliance permeated a vibrant place & people varied as the fauna

surrounding the great ochre river
coursing its way through this motherland

a people of regal blood
embodying beauty, power & wisdom
greeted her with smiling eyes

she saw different shades of black:
black like the wheels of time forever moving forward
black of ship's hulls survived
black of railroad tracks forged by hand
crude oil, fueling society with life's blood
black asphalt well trodden that maintains its composure
black soil feeding the deepest roots of ancient trees
shimmering black of sleek panthers stalking the jungle wild

the black of a universe unknown & ocean depths untapped
black musical notes scrawled on paper
singing melodies of sweet sadness
black of closed eyelids, colors of percolating dreams
not yet begun in sleep's passing
black fluid in an inkwell, full of stories yet untold

these images filled her thoughts
as she became aware of a familiar countenance
reflecting in her direction

she glimpsed her face
in the mirror
& for the first time
she smiled at her own image

THIRTEEN

Descent: Journey to the Underworld

wearing dark sunglasses
face hidden beneath a baseball hat
she thinks no one will notice her
believes her clever disguise aids her attempt
to appear a part of the stool by the dingy bar counter

fringes of her faded cut-off jeans
brush against her thighs with each leg crossing
successive popping sounds as she cracks each knuckle
one of two things is inevitable here;
she will either walk out pockets empty
or take a chance at "*easy money*"

a man, worn as his t-shirt, sits nearby
hoping the latest arrival
will be taking it all off today
he eyes the curve of her
imagines underneath the white tank top
sips his beer, licks suddenly dry lips
takes in the "off-limits" terrain
close enough to touch

his attention turns to the center of the room
where a tall, lamp-tanned brunette
wearing a neon green bikini
accompanied by 80's soft rock
leaps fierce into the air
grabs ahold towards the top of the pole
presses one hand to the ceiling
poses while repositioning the other hand behind her back
before descending slowly, a spiral of legs spread wide
she resembles a "y" intentionally unwinding
core strength & gravity leading her deliberately
back towards the raised platform
now carpeted in mostly one dollar bills

i am definitely not going to f*ck with the pole
the newcomer decides
wondering how she could learn to do that
considering playground bars at recess as distant experience
her former upper body strength is no longer applicable
but experience is not necessary
& when money & opportunity are scarce
cash paid daily equals survival

twenty something's to middle-aged men
step forward from the shadows
cast crumpled bills on the perimeter of the stage
relocate nearer to the fallen presidents
gaining a closer view to the untouchable

i can totally do this she assures herself
contemplating issues more pressing
than the fear of undressing before strangers
she calculates the number of shifts required
to pay rent, buy food & school supplies for her children,
keep the lights & phone on another month

drawn in by ads claiming hundreds a day are possible
breaking it down in theory the whole thing is simply mathematics
figures tonight she just needs enough for groceries
more nutritional than ramen & kool-aid
after all, she's been naked in front of lovers for free
how different can it be?
but it's simpler hypothetically than in reality

another drink helps numb internal contradictions
the deejay cues her musical selections
introduces the newcomer to the stage
as the familiar bass line drops
she ascends the handful of stairs

& begins

Woman Disregarded

from auction blocks & slavery
to a video ho economy
there has always been a price on my body
a claim on fertile territory
her-story erased & rewritten by his-story

the same plans that turned eden to wasteland
left bruises over pocket change with bare hands
seeking out new markets in which to expand
in order to propagate & dominate more women & land
while i faltered at the clinic
explaining the pregnancy was unplanned

daughter of baby's daddies who stayed gone
the one, no matter the circumstances, in the wrong
while rapists in power declare "let bygones be bygones"
& r kelly tops the charts with yet another song

& my life is that of a doormat walked
one who said "no thank you" & got stalked
begged for my life from a lover who held a gun cocked
a woman blamed for all sins when muthaf*ckas cast rocks
never seen again in juarez
after punching out on factory time clocks

bound, gagged, chained & padlocked
sh*t even bits of my body parts worn as ornaments
didn't cause enough shock
so i've been lost
selling flesh for dollars on city blocks
from childhood to death mocked

> *here i stand a woman disregarded*
> *tears cascade from my eyes*
> *will i go to my tomb broken hearted?*
> *along the way essential duality was violently parted*
> *seems to be no end for the trend now that it is started*

i've heard that life began with the breath of a kiss
read about societies worshipping the goddess
but somehow in our midst
it was forgotten that her face looked like this
societal downfall still blamed on eve
since many men fear loving women &
it is easier to dissect those
not viewed as holy or human

so my flesh burns at the stake
when others sense my power
my spirit trampled underfoot
like unappreciated flowers
flesh cleared away for the building
of more steel & phallic towers
13 moons forced to twelve
to negate earth cycles are ours

labeled a whore by descent
never having the benefit
of being innocent or virgin
sexual pleasure removed by surgeons
my image not represented as heaven sent but from hell
the weight of each so called sin making my belly swell

while folks around the globe destroy their baby girls
knowing there is little love for them in this world
& each woman is survivor & yet viewed at fault
while the madness & violence ceases to halt
what future lies on the horizon for the *man*kind we know
that leaves torn, battered, slaughtered women wherever it goes?

> *blood runs down my thighs my womb disregarded*
> *tears cascade from my eyes*
> *will i go to my tomb broken hearted?*
> *along the way essential duality was violently parted*
> *seems to be no end for the trend now that it is started*

Purple & Yellow

...walls scream in hostile houses
neighbors can't help but know
children go without sleep
women go to work with relocated noses
purple & yellow ribbons
cover cheeks & thighs
backs & shoulders
war wounds
but we won't talk about the undeclared wars. *

the ebb & flow of violence
returns home with more frequency
once a month "accidents"
prove difficult to hide
when they become constant blemishes
rotating locations
brightly colored markings
buried beneath reapplied foundation

today will bring unmapped tides of pain
perhaps after breakfast
when his egg yolk comes out broken
or his toast is burnt
he'll suspect an affair
when evening traffic
makes her 10 minutes late

sinkholes swallow households
families get stuck
what we prayed was passing weather
becomes a permanent condition
so we tread lightly
hoping not to draw attention to ourselves
stillness comes from absence
& bouts of unconsciousness bring brief
intermissions between rounds of rage

no longer resting at night
we drown into schizophrenic psyches
struggling to forget
mostly remembering
reliving daily nightmares

hope, a slight beam
penetrates the suffocating depths
fuels the desire to run

     run!
          run for your lives!

regardless of what our lovers tell us
we deserve better than this daily barrage
knuckles, knees, boots, bloody sinks
wall impressions left in plaster
where a head was slammed

desperate to run away we plan the departure
with every single thought of flight
but everything seems obvious
with someone constantly watching
peering over shoulders when we write
observing out of car windows
calling & checking in hourly
randomly appearing
face & fist hidden in every shadow
causing paranoia when we turn corners

so we know essential items locations
too suspicious when found together:
wallet, top drawer under pajamas
$20 sewn into the seam of a winter coat
$10 crushed into the toe of a boot
birth certificates & pocket address book
stashed in the filing cabinet beneath the electric bills
essential clothes in bottom drawers

& hidden in the jewelry box
on her daughter's dresser
sitting sideways are two quarters
phone calls when she flies

* from Moment of Silence
written by Good Sista/Bad Sista
Turiya Autry & Walidah Imarisha

Scattered Seeds

we are the seeds
cast throughout the world
some falling to asphalt
some to sea
a few to rich earth
others amidst weeds

sown, blown & torn
trying to blossom & bloom
without enough room
always getting plucked (f*ck)

petals smashed on the sidewalk
bleeding scent & color
aroma faded, stem wilted

the roses got smart
& grew thorns-
but even that was no match for scissors

Unnamed

skeletons scream from closets
always some man
a laying on of hands
minus the healing
leaving scars on the subconscious
blood on memories
pain that seeps
from the insides out
can't be shed with tears
or years of wanting to forget

statistics claim it's one in four
but it seems to knock
on every woman's door
in the form of the well dressed/ unshaven
college educated/ never graduated
city/country/suburban
red tied corporate thugs
wearing tailored shoes
boots or tennis shoes
we must be wary of them all

if almost every woman
has been victim to either:
dates, family, lovers, neighbors
only sometimes strangers
someone who *may* have been
next to us in line at the grocery store
beside us in class
at the front of the bus
with us on a date
living down the street
on our blocks, next door
in the next room

sometimes
nowhere seems safe
with women still being raped
of their compassion, childhoods, innocence
left bleeding in dark corners of society
while men
straighten their ties
tie their laces
zip their flies
& pass by

back to business as usual
ignoring trails of their transgressions
red marks we survivors wear
around our hearts & thoughts
knowing ncxt timcs are possible
men can be unstoppable
& pain plants doubts
fears & insecurities that take root
can't be weeded out or talked about

if we find ourselves
in the wrong place, wrong time
wrong circumstance
it is more than chance
these violations
are on purpose
intentional

_he_ did it
later pretending not to know
_he_ did it
we're the only ones that know
_he_ did it
without allowing an option to say no

but we say **_no more!_**

on behalf of our ancestors, our families
our friends, our neighbors, our children
we scream ***no more!***

because silence after
does not erase the blame
of attackers named & unnamed
who return back to the office
the house next door
the room down the hall
while tears still fall

worlds ripped apart
from the inside out
shattered on sidewalks & back seats
left bleeding in crumpled "princess" bed sheets
too many pieces to count
too much pain to ignore

Resurrecting Beauty

after 400 years without a comb
i began underestimating, negating
berating & degrading
my inner goddess
denied my connection
to the roots of nappiness & happiness
striving for a relaxed state
in the midst of self hate

i was constantly struggling to be something else
as if the face i wake up with
can't be the one i cherish
as if the body i live in is never
an accurate depiction of my aspiration

previously unaware that my hair
is an extension from the base of my thoughts
through & beyond spirals of this galaxy
this lifetime serving as a tool
to navigate the journey

i know the universe
holds more for me & we than this:
suffering & hunger, misdistribution of wealth
forcing survival to equal distance from the earth
gun-fire, destruction, prisons & war
drive thru lifestyles & convenience stores

colonizers decimated self-sustaining communities
still force-feed dependency & yes
i am yet another generation of addict
borrowing against my life
while debts owed
from blood soaked hands go unpaid

but we have not forgotten:
hysterical screams of kidnapped
vicious blows crippling backs
mothers stolen from babies
folks tied to train tracks
beaten for struggling

burning flesh & broken bones
nails through hands & crowns of thorns
we carry the pain of the earth
& attempt to save it
armed with slingshots & rocks
aiming for eyes
we alter sight, recreate vision
motivate changes in perception & direction
by skewing negative gravitations
emanating from forced relocations, manipulations
& the few constantly seeking domination

i regain my natural rhythms
& the spirals on my head
serve as antennas
picking up signals from the sun
reminding me that while hundreds of years
may mark empires
they are only a ripple
in this vast ocean of eternal time

so this lifespan of mine
is neither beginning nor end
just brief time passing
& there are many more
after & before me
than i can ever comprehend
supplying no end to this mathematical equation
of water & bone, flesh & dome
enabling me to use my vessel
as a tool to write another poem
knowing hours spent reflecting

& projecting positive energy
returns threefold & love
is cosmically unending
eternally limitless
& i am supplied in abundance

so i share it as a gift
to which all are entitled
without fine print, unbridled
because i know that we are more than this:
first impressions, products of rejection
deception & oppression
influenced by notions of the west
mistakes of fathers, spoils of robbers
conveying bitterness & weariness lacking sleep
trapped in worlds we did not create
that mark time with scars of rings cut deep

finally able to treat the wounds
with knowledge predating wisdom of carved runes
we begin that cataclysmic cipher
& bring dormant roots back to life

Crossroad Blues

hands tired of labor
want to make music
pick six strings
instead of cotton

nothing left to lose
he halts at the crossroads
prostrates himself at the juncture
indecision | desire - ambition | fear

esu & elders whisper
be careful what you wish for
unable to quiet legends
that satan gives favors

all paths leading from now
he mumbles incantations through trembling lips
calling the devil at midnight
to tune his sears & roebuck guitar

Grandpa Trickster

after weeks of counting in increments of 5
while sitting at the table of the sun
his earthly granddaughter
beat him at dominoes
when she was only 13
so he hurled all 28 bones into the sky
where they still shine on clear nights

he worked the rails while on land
to blend in with those considered common
knowing full well that saints
often beg on street corners to test for purity of heart
& atonement & benediction are found in juke joints
as often as churches, where true believers
drink spirits & holy water from the same glass

he diagnosed grief in his surroundings
& used humor as a panacea, curing pain with laughter
when medicines refused to mend wounds fully
prescribing black magic remedies deep fried
& seasoned with hot sauce

he captured hornet stings & barbs
in the thick skins of his soles
freed them with razorblades
hurling them at unsuspecting mortals
that underestimated the sharpness of speaking tongues

sometimes words are the only weapons available to gods on earth

Isis in Time of War

stones get hurled, dent tanks
bombs are thrown at living targets
people cry foul
seekers find

civilians fall
there is nothing civil
in war games
where people are cut losses
expendable casualties

with all the rubble falling
it is hard for peace talks
to make a difference
metal & flesh don't mix

tissue gives way to tear
people shattered in pieces
throughout the earth

i want to be like isis
gather them together
make them whole

but i don't know how she did it

Truth

captive cities
live behind razor wire
armed guards stand watch

　　　　　　　　　there are reasons
　　　　　　　　　why prison funding rises
　　　　　　　　　while social services decline
　　　　　　　　　slavery never ended

here, civilians are sardines
confined to small spaces
assigned showers
meals without sharp utensils

millions in limbo
without rights, votes or rehabilitation
hardening
adjusting
to life
on the inside

　　　　　　　　　take a number
　　　　　　　　　it is yours for a lifetime

standing by the fence
looking in
is a revolutionary
in search of stolen kin
she has come
to watch over them with empathy
she has come to set them free

in the face of towering walls
& armed guards
she carries the ultimate weapon

Unstoppable

my fingers freeze at the keys
when i attempted to type this
syllables seized on the tip of my lips
when i worried if you & your friends
might actually like this
spread wisdom & interest
incite riots & exodus
excite the local pacifists
turn toddlers into activists
get grandmas standing on corners
in the suburbs raising power-to-the-people fists

that's why i finally came to claim space on the stage
to bring words without hesitance
because not everyone will comprehend the relevance
unless the bloodshed & violence
lie within their specific circumference
& they are unfortunate enough to witness
with their own eyes
that precious life is too often wasted
& money & influence
can't always save us

when triggers squeeze
bended knees & pleas
can't stop a bullet
stitches, elbow grease & medicine
won't always cure the wounded
the best-laid plans are often ruined
but we must get through this
without blueprints
because challenges change
with each day & encounter

> *but together we are unstoppable & nothing is impossible*
> *together we are unstoppable & nothing is impossible*

another day on empty
manages to erase quickly
the feeling that i find
when i am still & delve into
the sub-conscious rawness in my mind
begging for exercise & ideas finally actualized
& while last days are prophesied
our actions today & tomorrow
impact outcomes not yet finalized

we are ancestral prayers realized
bound destinies untied redesigned
the difference in the air
strong like second-hand smoke
mixed with coffee grinds
when each & every one of us
decides to recognize

while theorists search through records
documents & statistics
others analyze complex dynamics
over blazed spliffs
& multitudes of people
keep coming with that real sh*t
so true to life you'd swear
you could just about taste it

  together we are unstoppable & nothing is impossible
  together we are unstoppable & nothing is impossible

Life Before Death

give me mine while i'm alive
i don't want flowers when i die
i want to relish in life & love hard
there may not be a second chance

i don't want a fancy tombstone
leaning in a field of millions
buried centuries deep in wanting
with a view to illusion
only to be buried again
under future civilizations

i don't want gold
a building named after me
books written about me decades later
when someone "discovers" me too late
i won't send my ear to my lover
then die hungry

i don't want to leave this chaos
knowing it will continue
its mad direction for eternity
my life making no difference

i want to live fulfilled
stand naked in the rain
while no one watches
free

nature's design bountiful enough for all
yet many go on with so little
having less than our share for centuries
this civilization
run by greedy children
who let the milk pour down their mouths
while the world goes hungry

salvaging crumbs & scraps are crimes
punishable by the laws of idolatry

god is not a white man
what's taught as truth is false
& answers are dying
with every tree cut down
that holds stories in its roots
every tombstone never inscribed
paved over graveyards of many
whose stories weren't written
weren't read, weren't passed on

don't wait to listen for my stories after i die

i want my love, happiness
gifts, appreciation, attention
my life now

don't bring me flowers when i die
i'll take mine while i live
huge bouquets, a planted garden
full spectrum, colorful centerpieces on tables
wooden boxes along the front porch
where neighbors care about & know each other
wild flowers in a field i can run through naked
under a full sun with a warm breeze

i don't want people to cry for me after i die
life is always too short
cry with me while i am here
because the world is cold
i long for warmth

wipe my tears today
hold my hand today
i want my love today

don't gather in mass when i'm gone
some grand number to shed tears in black
fill my house now
come together in life

don't wait until i am no more
to think of me with every passing day
as you've never thought of me before
i want my letters now, my attention now
give me my love now
because i am dying & i want to know it
while i am still alive

In Search of Osiris

four directions i traversed
looking for each fragment of my love
maimed & misplaced
across the land we ruled

his smile that sliced the dark sky with light
my tears creating chasms dividing nations
his arms spread too wide to take hold
my hands torn from carrying the weight of severed pieces
found throughout the shadows of hate
darkening each road i searched

how fast did set run with his body?
casting it to the sands of deserts
wet soil of marshes
as if my brother could ever be forgotten
when gods do not die

flesh torn asunder
i gather each limb
cradle them against my body
protecting memories
praying the sum of thirteen parts is enough

as i the unskilled surgeon
attempt to resurrect the dead
with bare hands & the magic they hold
it is our love, stronger than death itself
which makes us whole

We Dance

we drift between the loose edges
of our surroundings as if to blend in
there are none stranger here than we

i ease my way through the room
into the corners of your smile
i recognize you lover, we've passed before
reflected light of mutual inspiration
fond of words for volumes now
we craft poetry authors struggle to write
spilling over tongues & parted lips
sweet shared breath embraces
freed from inkwells unconfined by lines & pages

we pound rhythms of earth vibration
bared feet on wood floors
hips & hands & thighs keep time
winds scented clove
vanilla candles dripping waxed jazz
our rivers rising, filling rooms
with warm waters souls swim in

we flow to times pausing
reels un-captured by cameras
spreading beyond limitations of single frames
imaginations ignited, flames intertwine
blaze before open eyes

heat appears the color of skin
tastes of yearning
feels soft smooth
against tips of fingers
rubbing off layers
revealing moist earth glowing moonlight
reminders of selves realized
forgotten fragments
blended whole

On Wax

leaned against the wall next to the stereo
wax was my first love
each stack a history of transition & creation
soundtracks of our waking lives
crisscrossed in corduroys on shag carpet
i studied cover art

playing a record takes two hands
love & appreciation
slight handling with fingertips
coaxing records from paper linings
a laying down with grace
before precisely placing the needle

      rhythms also depend on silence

vinyl went underground & left me
playing double dutch after school on tape decks
grabbing song samples off the radio
dee-jaying cassettes in the living room
the wiry body of a child escaping structure
exercising choices making mix tapes

while my mother
just wanted to hear a single song
from beginning to end

Skipped

as soon as she hears the notes
before the skip on the track of "blue trane"
she knows it's coming
glaring squawk of electronic repetition
sounds that don't fit together
force her to search forward
past the smudged space

inevitably his lips move to form phrases she's heard
throughout various stages of relationships
& has come to know well

she predicts the next bar of the tune that begins with
> *you're beautiful & incredible...*
> *i will never meet anyone else like you...*

> *you know*
> *you know i*
> *you know i love you but...*
> *our tune is played out*
> *this band is breaking up*
> *i'm going solo*
> *you have fallen down the charts*
> *i have found a new number one*

> *i know this isn't what you want to hear*
> *i know this isn't what you want*
> *I know this...*

she tunes it out
waits for the next single
removes him out of rotation on the frequent play list
where she caressed his curves regular
fell asleep to the rhythms
of breaths & heartbeats

there are other LPs & CDs
my favorite things bringing her peace
cause she can enjoy herself
without some one-hit wonder
she doesn't need company
when she's got coltrane, candlelight
& a bed all to herself

Rwanda III: Umoja

we come together
brothers & sisters
who live at a distance
cherishing the reunion

we come together
bearing gifts of wisdom
dreams of peace
visions for a better future
celebrating the beauty
of our collective cultures
our unity a point of strength

we come together
our longing for freedom & justice
cannot go unanswered
our struggle & hard work
will not be in vain

we come together
a powerful force
like the tide of oceans
carving new channels
towards divine destiny

we come together
growing like multitudes of plants
covering fertile land finding harmony
within their varied purpose & place
giving sustenance

we come together
our love & energy spreading far & wide
throughout our communities into neighboring regions
bringing light & hope

we come together knowing the labor will be difficult
& the rewards immeasurable

Undercurrents

below the surface of calm
where waters grow dark
hidden insecurities gather
in hopes of never being discovered
turbulent eruptions of emotions
quieted by cold glass
lake layers of pretending

no one can plunge to the center of my earth
which lies unfathomed, beyond measure
& the grasp of the best divers
longing to pluck out
shiny mementos of the voyage
reminders of this unmapped truth

crowds gathered at the edges of my serenity
fear my depths, even after years of knowing
the geography of my countenance
they skip stones & cast lines
scratch the superficial
witness peacefulness
disturbed slightly in gentle ripples

once efforts sink beyond their reach
they abandon my scenery
for the company of other destinations

most of me hides in volcanic rocks
formed by fires of past lives
that left permanent marks
lava tears singeing as each one fell

the bottomless lake of my soul
proves only that i used to cry
saving each wet drop as a reminder
so people might venture in my direction
inquire about my feelings
buried deep down for so long
even i no longer know where to find them

Diving Lessons

i saw reflections of myself
glimmering gold against sunlight
didn't worry
about getting lost
once i got wet

took tips of toes
dipped metallic green black
across the surface
watched water spiral
& work its way
to the furthest edge
growing deeper still

the familiar faded
to distant shores
yet i considered myself
home adrift
on three parts water
buoyed on a fourth
of soft skin earth
trembling slightly
with the wind

i dove headfirst
into the depths of his eyes
pulse quickening
with the shock of the plunge
breath silenced
vision blurred

disoriented
i lost sight of land
forgot to hold my breath

No Take Backs

typical weekend afternoon:
ride dirt bikes
stop for snacks
play out back

adventurers marking our travels
with scattered innocence & the chatter
of playing cards between spokes
on a long short-cut

we made a discovery by a neighbor's shed

magazines thickened damp
stacked high, worn & weathered
curled on the corners
not intended for young audiences
sparked curiosity

we shouldn't have looked
didn't leave well enough alone
instead, compelled
we turned too many pages
images aimed below the belt
struck hard
knocked the wind out of lungs
left us speechless

> *is this what little girls are made of?*
> breasts crotch ass thighs
> vulnerable & exposed for strangers eyes
> *is that what little girls are made for?*

i wasn't ready to be discovered
by settlers heading west to go east
little boy explorers on long short-cuts
leaving soiled tracks as they made their way
across the plains of my body

pissing out boundaries
for new backyard territories
conquest & submission
the new daily activities
there are no take backs

decades later
I am still in recovery
mending battle scars
inflicted by raiding boys crying war

Reclamation

be independent again
we end the business of them
rewriting the script
taking out the rebellion
making it easy to swallow & follow
but thoroughly hollow
we are reclaiming our beats back
for the cause of revolution

i decide to put a halt in the co-opt
& take my music back, see
living a life without warranty
you gotta claim the now & know the why
cardboard boxes were necessary school supplies
for lunch time excursions
the art of the scratch on black wax tracks
amplified shoulder high through boom box blasts
got bodies contorting, creating motions
unseen before pop lockin
music got crowds flockin
& break dancing should've been an olympic sport
cause i saw folks shatter records of gravity & velocity
over concrete, but certain drumbeats continue to be outlawed
jim crow knowing a crowd with purpose causes problems
too many congregated slaves may spread ideas
involving more than hips, thighs & backsides
we code lyrics of overthrowing masters & freedom rides
our beats gain momentum as more understand them & join in
we head to the offices of music industry executives & say
this is a hold up muthaf*cka
& we've come for what's ours

we end the business of them
rewriting the script
taking out the rebellion
making it easy to follow & swallow
but thoroughly hollow

we are reclaiming our beats back
for the cause of revolution

corporates can no longer use them
go platinum off the backs of black folks then discard us
talking about how they work hard
& I guess jacking culture is hard work
& that's how they justify
paying themselves overtime
for stealing our rhymes
while we toil through the ages
for their minimum wages
but they aren't taking hip hop without a fight
it is rightfully ours
inherited from the roots of southern trees
scarred with the sound of whip cracks
music sung hushed in quarters
chanted over hammering train tracks
that soul, that rhythm, that blues, that jazz
that be-bopping, show stopping
crowd bobbing, head nodding
heart throbbing resistance
with a raised fist

be independent again
we end the business of them
rewriting the script taking out the rebellion
making it easy to follow & swallow
but thoroughly hollow
we are reclaiming our beats back
for the cause of revolution

Freedom & Justice Are Not Optional

ceo's sit in the lap of luxury tossing dollar bills around like confetti
while millions of the restless unite, stand up & get ready
we take the alcohol society's sippin'& light it on fire
no time to hesitate or procrastinate
we meditate on the flames growing higher & higher
birthing the phoenix the future desires & requires

our rebellions & riots won't be kept quiet
the status quo, you know, we will continually fight it
we won't be overpowered by showers of tokens & trinkets
or false advertising so don't bother to think it
miscellaneous distractions & rules
only fuel factions of puppets & fools
reacting to the latest trends
attempting to acquire more ends
relinquishing their better interest & giving in
to the lure, the latest instant cure
claiming to *"take all pains away"*
"make blue skies out of gray"
without altering the circumstances
we are subjected to day to day

it's a quick fix, a media blitz, a cover up of the real sh*t
made available by corporate sponsorships
marketed worldwide glamour & glitz
through appealing women in revealing outfits
who get paid to masquerade as dimwits
perpetuating stereotypes of being ready
willing & able to submit
minimizing the extent of our existence
so i encourage your resistance

but provocative operatives attempt to nullify positive actions
using underhanded tactics to fuel our reactions
incentives are given to mollify the middle classes
who avoid exploring their own conditions
listen,

it's the difference in force
between a single teardrop & an ocean
when we're insistent that simply "more"
is not enough or an option

yet indulgence is inherent within the system
our inhibitions are considered weakness
so we do what's necessary for acceptance
& entrance into our own oppression
we venerate our master's wishes with deference
following fear & ignoring historical references
buried within the pages of western rhetorical texts
repeating washed & worn cycles
depleting resources & vitals
our minds, bodies & spirits remain idle
stuck on maintaining the basics of survival

we succumb to the weight of the chains
slow down the pace of the blood through our veins
& remain calm
victim to the routine inequity
of a world power still in infancy
where acquiescence of consciousness is insisted
since thought causes interference
& probability of resistance

ignorance is seen as a state of awareness
& it all seems to make perfect sense
since we contain, retain the sickness & indulge it
silent witness to the epidemic apathy
towards atrocities unfolded
we're scolded for challenging the status quo
kids grow & learn young to go with the flow
so behold the degradation of the new age
wage slave of the modern corporation
& let's hasten the determination
& steps we take
to actualize freedom

Untitled

your attention is divine
a savored flavor & first choice
since i envy your voice
spending all day moist
in your mouth
upon lips & tongue
the scripts undone
& once begun
i find myself poet sprung
so with each kiss & sweet experience
remember this:

in my random thoughts I occupy time
considering how many ways
we could make love, without ever having sex
images form instantly like a natural reflex
my mind visualizes
hands & oils, mouths & flavors
tongues tasting, time savored
chocolate painting & foreplay for hours
full body massage & candle lit showers
clothed grinds like high school endeavors
pleasure unmeasured
performance style exhibition
a classic rendition
long awaited fantasy
between you & me
a camera, a mirror
passion with fervor
where i watch your expressions
let loose without repression

my sweet, i have a confession
you need not fear rejection
cause what i most humbly request
is an opportunity to say "yes"

Stow Away Love

what will you do with my love
if i stash it under your pillows
so it caresses your dreams
in the form of lingering kisses?

maybe i should hide it in your suitcase
so it can follow you home
move in with you
a quiet roommate
brightening your house like sunshine

i could hand it over in person
wrapped in insecurities & pink ribbons
i could whisper it before you wake
to avoid the risk of rejection

i could be stingy with my love
keep it all to myself
but it has no value
hidden in secret thoughts
unexpressed

i could write it down
fold it up
place it in your pocket
so you could keep it close
cherish it, acknowledge its existence

would it be just ink on paper
flat without inspiration or
would it move you to feel the same?

Mental Masturbation

i would love you like redwoods
tall, roots running deep
arms open wide

i would love you like flowers
soft colorful petals blooming
to meet the sunshine of eyes
soft caress of fingertips

i would love you like mangoes
lips tasting & relishing
sticky & wet

i would love you like racing my bike
hot breath filling my lungs
cool breeze floating through my hair
caressing my face as i reach hilltops
slide down crescendos

i would love you like nighttime
dark, mysterious
nocturnal cravings
wandering, roaming
places unseen

i would love you like honey
slowly flowing
delicate
golden

i would love you like winter sweaters
snug & warm
comforting & soft
wrapped round your chest

i would love you like heartbeats
rhythmic, pounding, pulsating
deep within me

could i love you like dreams
filling your thoughts
& your bed
with fantasy?

could i love you like butterflies
landing & pausing
spreading wings to fly
then color the sky?

could i love you like words
mouth parting, tongue lifting
lips curving, soft sounds
alighting your ears
transforming in your mind?

could i love you like chocolate
savoring you my sweet
as you melt on my tongue
saving some for later?

could i love you like diamonds
buried treasure
in the rough
found & polished
by skilled hands?

could i love you like grassy meadows
roll in you
lay down on you
feel moist comfort
all over my body?

could i love you like ocean
waves that lick ankles

work their way upwards
remove all my clothes
dive in?

could i love you like a movie star
afraid of washing off your touch
infatuated, obsessed
pictures of you plastered
on my bedroom walls?

if you were here
i would eat dessert off your chest
hot fudge sundae
whipped cream, cherries

if you were here,
i would dance for you,
stripping off layers
an encore or two

i would lay you in my bed
& tie your hands & feet with satin scarves,
(just loose enough for you to break free)
while i stroked your skin
with feathers of peacocks

i would take my index finger
trace the lines of your lips
the space in-between
awaiting the feel of tongue
on my fingers, up my arms, my shoulders
lingering on my neck

soft sensuous hands
explore lush eden gardens
making me moan ecstatic

could i love you
all life long?

since you aren't here
i have to settle for a hot shower
pretend the streams of water
are your kisses
washing over my body

pretend the hands that caress me
beneath the blankets
are yours & not my own

Sacred Sex

eternal oasis resides
the expanse of tempting thighs
delivering natural highs
nectar offerings rendered sweetly
kisses bestowed freely
renewing bodies completely
words whispered quietly
breath tickling ears slightly
as lost souls find each other nightly

in nocturnal raptures
the spirit captured speaks in tongues
erases scars when sung
caresses flesh's fantasies
parted lips, parted seas
heaven's earthly scent
holy space & sacrament
blessings of multiple forms
come in forty day & night storms
swaddled in layers of salvation
to keep warm

mind, body, spirit rejuvenation
elevating nations
nourishment of poetry
syllables are sustenance
healing hands inspire wide-eyed contact
soul search terrains of thought
where wild imaginations find waking dreamers
architects of the next life
free will wandering levels of consciousness

my love,
you are a constellation of fallen stars
tides of tenderness calling the sun to rise each morning

sculpt moons until daybreak
hum hymns & write scriptures of creation
deliberate inscriptions describing predictions
on the walls of my womb
where there is enough room
for all of your stories to be recorded

Dreams Dying of Thirst

burnt out on being burned
i am afraid to get too close
but dancing flames mesmerize
i crave the heat
seem to like playing with fire

then i realize i too am the flame
licking passion on the wind
maybe we will linger
leave ashy trails on sidewalks
searing kisses in alleys
then fade to dust

we could smolder
light torches for each other
stand on sunsets painting the future
orange & passion blaze
'til dusk covers brilliance
& day's glow retreats

nights don't have to be cold
the dark is not as frightening
with a candle & company
i hold a lighter
you bring the smile
emotions kindle
maybe we get burned

i can be so cool
cause folks to halt in their tracks
dare not confront me, if i chose
but frozen hearts
take too long to thaw

i'd rather be the cold cloth
easing scalding pain away

or be the cube of ice
melting on a sweltering lover
"thank god for lips"
that we might kiss again
ignite feelings lying dusty
on the back shelves of our imaginations
fearless of falling

i keep dreams & drink wishes
hope change lights darkened pathways
springs from winter into fields of possibility
bright on the horizon
futures well nurtured
rooted in loving smiles
soaked in compassion

i cannot let my visions perish of a starved soul
hearts wounded heal slowly
reopened too often before mending
but love wells up inside me
begs release or threatens self destruction
not able to accept being alone for long
twitching restless
tugging at my concentration
unsatisfied & unmatched
in attentive devotions

my heart is tired
laden down with tears unwept
painful histories kept & concealed
ready to fire like loaded weapons
found by children
then accidentally aimed

who will hold me
through nightmares
lying alone, scared into a hot sweat
the world breathes down my shoulders
powerful as houston heat in august?

who will know to dry my tears
when i claim it is only dust?
this damned flood
threatens to upturn
everything in its wake
just for want of attention

warning lights flash empty
on this journey of desolation
down an unlit highway
yearning for campfire & company
surrounded by desert
running out of water
as last tears are swallowed
from memories canteen

i scream silent
hold on to sanity
grip the edge of reality, tightly
hoping someone will feel me

Parting Gifts

my lover gives me parting gifts
to ease the pain of knowing
what we have is now over
thanks me for understanding
gives me a peck on the lips
a warm friendly hug
that lingers just a pinch
on the same couch
in the same room
we once set on fire with our heat
in a past life
before i'm informed
there is a new girlfriend

my lover felt it best
to tell me in person
after eight months since the first time we made love
after forty-three handwritten letters
after four months of their being together
after regular phone calls
after considering moving closer
since we both know long-distance is difficult
after i thought this might be "the one"
after my fiending
imagining wild nights of passion
filled with multiple orgasms
after i put on sexy underwear
& perfumed the parts
only the explorer would discover

after taking me out to dinner
telling me how incredible i am
how strong the love is between us
i felt certain
my drought was finally ending
but my lover gave me parting gifts!
gathered from various corners of the house
items i will appreciate later

once the pain is gone
wearing my everything's fine mask
i retreat to the realm of friendship
holding two spoken word CD's, a book
a small white box containing a pair of earrings
hand-crafted in some southwestern state

f*cking parting gifts!
when i thought
we'd be parting lips
legs & blankets
anticipating a night long ride to euphoria
destination coming together
squalls of desire brought on by hands
that know how to play my body
the way john plays the hell out of a horn
the way monk lays hands on keys
the way nina bends each sound
covering the entire scale
fury of emotion, striking each note with accuracy
artists crafting masterpieces of flesh

i was introduced to pleasures
my body had never met before
in that same room
on the same couch
now i grit my teeth
through a smile
my face no longer feels
conceal emotions non-friendly
rage & desire
as my lover gives me parting gifts
two spoken word CDs
poets i had never heard
a book of verse
a pair of earrings, hand-crafted
in some southwestern state
a kiss on the cheek
a hug

before sending me home

Language Acquisition

i chew your language awkwardly in my mouth
without the palate to translate a tongue i never learned
i butcher a short phrase with my serrated attempt
knowing nothing of your lullabies or bedtime stories
my sweet whispers are coated
in the syntax of our oppression
semantics of thieves who hijacked history

how different it must feel to say "i love you" in Shona

Lacuna

wrapped in ennui & frustration
mundane details of daily requirements
depression hangs gray & chill in the sky around me
blows through the empty spaces left from friends' departures
not yet recovered from the length of winter, spring finds me aching
my previous stars shining over cities too removed to touch

i want to fly & enfold distance
beneath wing spans wide enough to reach their light
remember joys pre-seeding today's monotony
recreate past lives to swallow this worn present

mind relaxed, imagination wanders on a deep exhale
lifted beyond the ceilings of classrooms & corporations
current events & miscellaneous frustrations
i find refuge in memories of love
the anticipation & reward of nights spent awake
daydreams beneath fickle moods of sun & sky at noon
a world drenched in honey coated midnights

letting go of tense, the past is present is future
nurturing crescent moons of white pearls
tomorrow becomes yesterday & tonight
dreams fill the void routine left behind
covering grays with violets
& autumns steeped in jasmine

Highway One: South

stars saturate the sky
brightening the darkness of midnight
mountainous black silhouettes
cover the view on the driver's side
giants standing guard
over the valley

i have climbed those hills by day
slowly winding along
gradually rising upwards
until near enough to the top
to kiss the fog & see the other side
stretch before me

the only way to come back down is to run
with a wide stance & a prayer

Los Angeles   *342 miles*

no other headlights expose the road ahead
every turn is a mystery
unfolding under high beams
causing drivers to appreciate the view
with caution

we are creeping our way
along the pacific
taking deep breaths upon gazing right

the white crests of ocean waves
a stark contrast against dark waters
reflecting moonlight hundreds of feet below
jagged cliffs mark the end of earth & road
keeping tides at bay

don't look down
drive with your eyes on the centerline

        Los Angeles   *339 miles*

an arched white bridge
covers the expanse of a chasm
carved where rivers return to sea
this beautiful & narrow structure rises
only to further uphold magnificence
not created by man

we are a traveling speck
on a lingering road between wonders

night still lies heavy outside the windows
mist rolls on land making it difficult
to see the distance that lies yards ahead & below

i have lit fires along the sandy northward shores
by nightfall removed my layers & plunged
towards this coastline's cold cobalt depths
without fear

friends I've had
chose to do the same
from the cliffs

don't look down
its hypnotic rhythms
will overwhelm

hours meander past
getting closer to the divine
making little progress towards anaheim

        Los Angeles   *333 miles*

Mathematics of the Heart:
How Does Love Function?

is it the square root of the number of times
i have handed my heart to someone
then watched it stomped to oblivion
+ Y, which = the number of folks
who proceeded to drop the remainders
inconsequentially by the roadside?

no, higher orders of operations
guide this equation called love
parenthetically hidden in every phrase between lines
exponentially expanding within my spirit
multiplying in magnitude & strength
i'm divided by constraints of time
additionally perplexed by the impact caused
when your company is taken away

square each & every drop of concentrated happiness
to the nth power, balanced on both sides
so your love & my love are equivalent
& infinite like the signature of pi
incongruent with limited physics of space & geography
proving our two bodies are actually able
to occupy the same space & time

our lowest common denominators
& fractioned shards of self
combined prove greater than the sum of parts
i've inked with answers in preparation for the unexpected
cause i want us to raise the curve on life's daily examinations
then rest on the crest of the highest point of joy
like shiny golden stars

Tasks to Finish Within My Mother's Lifetime

i carry dreams tied tight to my spirit
i am carrying mother's dreams
tied tight

seamed with patches
of our hued pasts
feet weighted with mud
together we are walking childhood's tracks
towards sunlight futures
sharing visions held tender
close as whispers between young girls
told they're supposed to be sleeping
but we're not sleeping
awake & alive today
we write rainbows across the sky with words

this time
is ours

we were conjured in hushed conversations
born of a mission through red tides
bearing gifts of change
wrapped in wishes & longing
held in palms & arms
under falling teardrops
chanted in mothers' prayers
to warm the fire next time
sealed in love
then sent into the world

Garden Gatherings of Gorgons

warned of wicked ones coming
we gathered women warriors
wisdom & arrows
fierceness & stone stares
amulets & spell casters to protect
pomegranate promises of immortality
& sacred wisdom shrines

the gardens only invited could taste
were eventually encircled
with haphazardly placed statues
clear warnings for future irreverent trespassers
to remember their place
in the presence of the goddess

Crack's In the Hallway

did they tell you heaven & hell
are places we reach after we die?

well the underworld is now
& eve could not find paradise
no matter how high
with one hit to the veins
she embarked on celestial plains
where the pain & the grays
fade

all that she's forgotten
had to be left behind
she's looking for light
a few bright stars
to guide her
so she can leave this world
& her own body

hypes say heaven is a hit on some good sh*t
but hell is the waiting room to get more
hypes say heaven is a pipe & a match lit
but hell is the jonz between scores

& she's falling
nothing to catch her
but concrete

falling
can't seem
to stay
on her
feet

door locked, lights out
he lays on the top bunk trying to sleep
ignoring the sounds

voices of addicted minds
wandering the hallway
smells of burning spoons
over oven-eyes
cradling drops of death

door locked
lights out
wishing to be anywhere
other than here
wanting to know the woman
who brought him into this world
but she is distant, with them
blended into the noises & footsteps
outside his doorway
treading back & forth, in & out
different voices seeking their turn
at white realities

you took too much!
scuffling, thuds, anger
then the sound of a deep inhale

> *with one hit to the veins*
> *they embark on celestial plains*
> *where the pain & the grays*
> *fade*

lost souls escaping life
through smoke & mirrors

door locked
lights out
waiting for morning
praying when he wakes up
it will be mom at the door
smiling with eyes of this world
knowing that she gave him life for a reason
wanting to hold him & give him her love

but cold in the kitchen
she holds her hands out to catch the fire
thinking of only one thing
becoming scarcer with each & every lighter flame

the first of the month becomes the second
the sun begins its ascent over lakeview
where houses are stacked like boxes
& still neighbors are strangers
echoes scurry from hallways
blend in with the streets & daylight

his door still locked
he barely slept
but maybe this morning
when she sees him
she will whisper she loves him
reminisce on how as a child he:

      learned to walk too young
      & bowed his legs

          spoke his first words
          as a complete sentence
          he waited 3 years to share

              came home soaking wet
              after riding his big wheel
              through a lake of puddles
              in his sunday's best

during these brief moments of clarity
when the highs replace lows & find quiet
he sees a glimmer of the woman
his mother once was
& imagines the times
before the addiction
& all the voices in the hallway

Cycles

we had been there before, her & i
in places of turbulence & tears
by the sides of hospital beds
crying, praying, gently touching fingers, palms
avoiding iv tubes, fresh wounds
machinery keeping bodies
just outside the doorways of death
& we walked through that opening
souls looking down on flesh left behind

but at age three i retraced those steps
followed the shine of daffodils
the feel of hands & sounds of a familiar voice
i found my way back
when doctors warned i wouldn't make it
or might never understand words
or walk again

we had been there before, her & i
in places where circumstances demand action
tears fall too frequently & pain is more
than we felt we could bear
we revisit the place
where weak find strength
to do the impossible
step out on faith
because that's all they have left

for all the time we couldn't spend together
every abbreviated kiss, missed phone call
for the book you never found the energy to write
the unfinished paintings & dreams deferred

i am sorry
we didn't deserve it
but we had been there before

sitting close as hospital beds allowed
holding hands, holding back fears
i worried she would lose her words
when she still had volumes to say
i wasn't ready to face her mortality
hoped she would run free
on legs that once knew how to walk

we had been there before, her & i

the day they finally let me return home
after months of intensive care, multiple surgeries
with a body whittled away to half its original self
but i was walking
i could talk
i was alive

miracles do happen
& mom must have known there was a god
when her prayers were finally answered
& i worry that i didn't know the right prayers
since she failed to get better

but i sat by the side of her bed
knowing we are not promised tomorrow
& we are never prepared for the worst

but we had been there before

relying on the warmth of each others love
finding ways out of difficulty
strong women, independent women
so often needing someone
only to find ourselves alone

& i remember being alone in the hospital
a child crying to sterile white walls
that couldn't brighten my spirits
my heart never forgot the isolation

when visitors got scarce
the sun of my days was her face
her smile, her touch, her warmth
& it saved me

once i was finally grown & on my own
she should've been able to enjoy her days
race after grandchildren,
giving them all the sweets
their hands could hold
not trapped in bed confined to a house
that turned on itself, began breaking down
doctors never had solutions, just prescriptions
that didn't slow the condition, or make her better

& on my mother's final night
they recommended i let her go
allow them to take her off the machines
as if i could give up hope
regardless of the monitor's declarations
& doctor's description of the inevitable

we had been there before, her & i

i envisioned her return
to the sound of my voice
the wetness of my tears
a victorious underdog battle
an individual determined
against all odds
she made the final decision
for herself

i didn't want to let go

but now her spirit bathes in ocean
drinks sunset while dancing on foamy waters
she has found the space to run free

Learning to Fly

i knew what it meant to fall
there's no time to grab a parachute
read every chapter in the "How to Survive
Worst Case Scenarios" handbook
gifted by your best friend in case of emergencies
cause she knew that sh*t can go real wrong

i went from meander to sprint towards the ledge
like Flo Jo with a flash of nails & blur of color
like dancing streaks of blue angels
faster than wind
fearless

& i knew what it meant to fall

what it meant to travel at c
700 million mile an hour hurtling
believing in the unseen
stepping out on faith knowing
there would be no bottom & no ending
assuming everything would be fine
if i could trust

so i chose to risk the sky
stretch my arms wide, open my heart
fill my lungs & reach to heaven
like Dr. Jemison, like Earhart, like Milkman
i chose to surrender to the wind
& let go

i knew what it meant to fall

& i learned:
that you can't return to the same place twice, exactly the same
moments of bliss are well worth the time it takes to mend
& my heart's forged stronger
having visioned beyond the horizon

realizing nothing of my imagination
is outside the grasp of my two hands
my own tongue ripe with the harvest
i laughed when i leapt
tasting freedom in the yield

i knew what it meant to fall

& i descended with inevitable gravity
waiting for hands to catch me
a several story cushion to magically appear
invisible strings to suddenly present themselves
i prayed, if i hit ocean, that my notebook
would serve as a flotation device

fear taunted me & doubt scolded me for taking risks
but what point is there in regretting what we can't take back?
i sung what i thought might be my last
knowing some stunts cannot be repeated
i closed my eyes, waiting for the sound of shatter

i knew what it meant to fall
& my OWN love caught me, reminding me
that i have always known how to fly

About the Author

Whether directing youth programs, teaching, rocking the mic or working behind the scenes, Turiya Autry is a positive motivational force. Through her work she encourages people to look more critically & lovingly upon the world around them.

For fifteen years she's taught & inspired children, teens & adults. As a teaching artist, she's provided hundreds of assemblies, workshops & residencies to over fifty different schools K-12. She's taught fifteen unique university courses, totaling over 200 credit hours, across four departments at Portland State University: Black Studies, English, Freshman Inquiry & Women, Gender & Sexuality Studies.

Turiya's featured at hundreds of venues & at over twenty colleges. He's toured nationally & performed internationally, as an individual performer, half of the dynamic duo Good Sista/Bad Sista & through other collaborations.

Turiya's opened for well known figures like Angela Davis, bell hooks, John Trudell, Nikki Giovanni, Ursula Le Guin, Spearhead, Saul Williams, Kevin Garnett & Hillary Clinton. Her recently released collection of poetry, ***Roots, Reality & Rhyme*** is a poetic journey that bridges the personal & political, the mythic & the real.

Appreciations

First and foremost, appreciations to the Ancestors & Elders as well as the universal force that enables me to exist & create.

Thanks to:
ALL OF MY FAMILY- for the support, love, insights, imperfections, lessons, talents & genetic material. Love to my Grandma Alice, my aunts & uncles, all of my cousins, nieces, nephews, in-laws & godchildren.

Amber, BethAny, Brian, Sage & Sharon- Were it not for close family & friends like them, I would not have been able to tour & perform in the world & grow my art. I appreciate their consistent loving support over the years. There are not enough words to express my gratitude.

Aunt Jean- When I most needed someone, she was there for me with love & caring that provided the foundation for me to flourish in the NW.

Christa Bell- Her advice & insights shed light & provide clear paths of action when I feel lost. She's remained a force in my life, since I was 18.

Dad- He showed up for me & has remained a consistent, reliable, loving presence in my life. I thank him for reminding me there are many paths to choose from & to pick my battles wisely.

Lola- I thought I was destined to be an only child. Thankful she came along to be a terrific sister and grow up alongside my children.

Mic Crenshaw- A big brother the universe gifted me on this artistic journey. His friendship, creativity, intellect & dedication inspire me.

Vagabond- He shares his amazing multi-media talents & insights to support others & inform. The cover art he created is absolutely perfect.

Walidah Imarisha- I'm amazed & impressed by all she manages to do, her brilliance & her sense of humor. Together we've taken on the stage, classrooms, the road & the world. So glad to have her in my life.

Also thanks to: (in no particular order)

Mo Fee, Cristina Orbe, Blacque Butterfly, Toni Hill, Ro Deezy, Auditory Sculpture, Seaside Slim, Boots Riley & THE COUP, Imani Muhammad, DJ Ian Head, David Walker, Jana & Audrey Love Crenshaw, The Lifesavas, Susan Addy & OALP, Al Letson, Dee Vance Warner, Damali Ayo, Invincible, Bryonn Bain, Carlos Andrés Gomez, Saul Williams, S. Renee Mitchell, Pam the Funkstress, Syndel, Bao Phi, Gabriel Teodros, Khingz, Zulu Nation 503 & 206, OPB, KBOO, Deena B, Nick Meisle, Opio Sokoni, Claire Oliveros, Steve Morozumi, Cheeraz Gorman, Seth Mulliken, Yves Le Meitour, Gen. Erik, John Ashford, Dee Vance Wagner, Leah & Rena Dunbar, Karima, Dan Shea, Mario Hardy, The Lathans, Meklit Hadero, Alixa & Naima of Climbing PoeTree, Sonia Whittle, Nazelah Jamison, Nisa Ahmad, Kween, Pam Phan, Avel Gordly, Sunshine Dixon, Terrance Scott, Anthony Sanchez, Gloria & O.B. Hill & the former Reflections Bookstore, Hakim Muhammad,
The Ed Team: Moon Rock, Pot Roast, RAM, Sylvan & Yarrow plus the Caldera staff & all the youth workers/artists & folks that I've known through the program, Joanna Rose, Shannon Wasson, Ladies First Collective in Seattle, Chill Will, Gordy Toyoma, Sandra de Helen, Ithica Tell, Public Enemy, Solena Rawdah, Kevin Sampsell, Catón Lyles, Tom McKenna, Tony Wolk, Alix Olson, Wendy Thompson, Writer's in the Schools, Young Audiences, Community of Writers, Carol Franks (r.i.p), Doria Roberts, Wone, OG-1, Rose Bent, Rob G, Kindu & Sayeed, Blue Scholars, I Was Born with Two Tongues, Staceyann Chin, Marc Bahmuti Joseph, Charles Ellik, Floyd Boykin Jr. & SpokenVizions Magazine, IPRC, Lynn Griffin, Nancy Sullivan, Phreewil, The Fosters, The B.O.P. Crew: Jess, Em, Jen, Krista, Spring, Rai (r.i.p.), Adam & the Roach Family, John & Karen Flaherty, Jesse & the Alinders, Laura Watson, Shawn Eaves, Amy McKee Sarty, Heatherlee, Rayaya, Oba, Miazia, The Autry Fam, Lynn Griffin, The Najiebs, Ken Green, Frosti, Black Studies at PSU & SFSU, Maria & Nikki De Priest, Susan Reese, Primus St. John, Dramaine Irion, Mandisa Fabris, Aisha, the MRAMs crew & FRINQ, Elisa Makunga, A.J. Lambert, Amy Hayes, Caralee Anley, Scott Parker, Barbara Horton Linn, Gilbert Crumble, Priya Kapoor, Tracy & Grace Dillon, Judith Patton, Candyce Reynolds, Scott Parker, Yves Labissiere, Denise Schmidt, Jena Johnson, Paul West (r.i.p)

To all the beautiful people, not mentioned above, who've: shared memories, supported my art, shared their art & have otherwise inspired me & made life more bearable: thank you.

93

A note about the timing of the book release...

The release of the long awaited Roots, Reality & Rhyme was timed to coincide with the 7 year anniversary of my mother's passing. My mom was my biggest fan & my own personal cheerleading squad. She supported all my dreams & ambitions, even when they changed overnight.

My mother suffered diminished health & mobility from a debilitative/degenerative case of MS, which she battled for many years. One day, just after the holidays, she went into a coma & was taken to the hospital. I rushed to see her, because the doctors were clear that it was just a matter of time. When I arrived, the doctors wanted me, as her power of attorney, to give them permission to take her off of life support. I couldn't do it.

Instead... I held her hand & read to her from my MA thesis, which I was scheduled to present & defend that term. A manuscript of poetry. She left this realm early the next morning, before I had to make the final decision.

It was the Sunday before winter term began. I cancelled teaching my university classes that week & focused on funeral arrangements, writing her obituary, notifying family & friends, being strong, breaking the news to my children & generally attempting to keep it together. A week after her departure, I was back to teaching. That same term, I defended my thesis & graduated. Didn't really have adequate time to mourn, because working class folks don't get to take time off to process the death of a parent- bills don't care about your personal life.

What I couldn't predict was the effect that association would have on my ability to release this book to the wider public. I would ask myself, "Why am I still sitting on this project?!" I understood and fathomed the connection only recently. Finally, I knew it was time. Remembering & marking the loss of my beloved mother, by celebrating life & finally birthing this project, created a motivating deadline. Thank you mom, for inspiring me still.